SIGNED: A NORMA

SIGNED: A NORMAL SINGLE MOM

Written By
Simona Titone

SIGNED: A NORMAL SINGLE MOM

SIGNED: A NORMAL SINGLE MOM

Copyright © 2024 Simona Titone

All rights reserved. No part of this book may be reproduced, or stored in a retrieval system, or transmitted in any form or by any means, electronic, mechanical, photocopying, recording or otherwise, without express written permission of the publisher.

This book is a work of non-fiction. The views expressed are solely those of the author and do not necessarily reflect the views of the publisher, and the publisher hereby disclaims any responsibility for them.

ISBN:

SIGNED: A NORMAL SINGLE MOM

SIGNED: A NORMAL SINGLE MOM

DEDICATION

This book is dedicated to my four lovely, caring, respectful, responsible, grateful, gorgeous, kind children, who have been – every day, since the first day of motherhood – my reason to live.

SIGNED: A NORMAL SINGLE MOM

SIGNED: A NORMAL SINGLE MOM

ACKNOWLEDGEMENTS

I would like to thank my amazing kids for choosing me as their Mom.

I would also like to thank my fantastic editor, Jessica Grace Coleman, the fairy who made it possible – with her kindness, professionalism, and constant patience – to transform my Still-Italian-sounding manuscript into a lovely book my readers can enjoy. You, Jess, made my dream come true.

And I would like to thank Matt Rudnitsky, the author who – on an Autumn morning by the sea – lit in me the spark to write again.

Without any of these six amazing people, my book would not exist, so I thank them all in the same way with a warm Mom's hug.

I will be forever grateful to Alena Kalchanka - the incredible artist whose motherly love and passion for painting with her heart made it possible for me to have the best book cover ever.

And dear Salman, you are my cherry on the cake.

SIGNED: A NORMAL SINGLE MOM

SIGNED: A NORMAL SINGLE MOM

TABLE OF CONTENT

CHAPTER ONE: Nice To Meet You 13

CHAPTER TWO: What Do You Mean…Normal? 17

CHAPTER THREE: I Am Trying 25

CHAPTER FOUR : Let's Learn 29

CHAPTER FIVE: My Physical Condition 33

CHAPTER SIX : Ehi, I've Got Remedies! 37

CHAPTER SEVEN: Let's Stay Healthy 43

CHAPTER EIGHT: A Poem To My Kids 45

CHAPTER NINE: No Plans Today 49

CHAPTER TEN : My Hamster 51

CHAPTER ELEVEN: A Funny Quote 55

SIGNED: A NORMAL SINGLE MOM

CHAPTER TWELVE : A Nice Place To Be 57

CHAPTER THIRTEEN: The Guy (Not 'The Gay').. 59

CHAPTER FOURTEEN: Go To Your Death Bed One Sec, Not Joking 63

CHAPTER FIFTEEN: Writing A Book......................71

CHAPTER SIXTEEN: This Page Is All For You 75

CHAPTER SEVENTEEN: I Could Cry 77

CHAPTER EIGHTEEN: Pumpkin Spice Latte 79

CHAPTER NINETEEN: My Yoga 83

CHAPTER TWENTY: Beetroot Crisps Petition 87

CHAPTER TWENTY-ONE: Yes, Or No? 89

CHAPTER TWENTY-TWO: It Can Only Happen In Brighton (I Think) 91

CHAPTER TWENTY-THREE: To The Fathers Who

SIGNED: A NORMAL SINGLE MOM

Do Not Financially Support Their Kids, Using Any Personal Justification They Can Come Up With, Thinking That Maybe Today Their Kids Don't Need Any Food Or Clothes 95

CHAPTER TWENTY-FOUR: I Want It Cut Really Short 97

CHAPTER TWENTY-FIVE: Thoughts 101

CHAPTER TWENTY-SIX: The Lonely Moments ... 103

CHAPTER TWENTY-SEVEN: My Mom 107

CHAPTER TWENTY-EIGHT: Child Anxiety 111

CHAPTER TWENTY-NINE: What Else Shall I Wish For? 113

CHAPTER THIRTY: Let It All Go 115

CHAPTER THIRTY-ONE: We Should Speak More 119

CHAPTER THIRTY-TWO: A Yoga Principle 123

CHAPTER THIRTY-THREE: I Just Wanted To Let You Know 125

CHAPTER THIRTY-FOUR: I Hear You 127

CHAPTER THIRTY-FIVE: Let's Reframe Everything 131

CHAPTER THIRTY-SIX: What If? 135

REFERENCE LIST 139

BIOGRAPHY 141

SIGNED: A NORMAL SINGLE MOM

CHAPTER ONE

NICE TO MEET YOU

Well, it didn't go exactly as I'd planned when I was young, but here I am.

I've been described as 'self-determined, strong, sweet, loving, kind and on a constant journey of self-improvement'.

Nice to meet you. I am a single mom.

And I mean a 'normal' single mom. The 'how do-I-get-to-the-end-of-the-month' one.

The one thinking, *Don't you dare roll your eyes or even think about not hiring me because I'm a single mom – I have fewer absence days in my working history than all of the young people you have on board put together.*

I am not an expert, and this is not a 'how-to' book.

But if there is something I can write about, it's being a single mom. After raising four children and seeing how happy they turned out… yes, I can say that.

If you're also part of this team, you'll know what I'm talking about. We belong to that extraordinary percentile of humanity, proudly carrying that unconditional loving heart of a mom – and the balls of a man.

This is a 'Let's Share' book, coming from the heart and exploring the truth of everyday life. It's a way to let you know you're not alone, and that – no matter what they might think – nobody is perfect.

So, are you looking for someone who finally understands those thoughts, or simply someone to share them with? Are you ready for some good thought-provoking questions along the way? And maybe a couple of interesting details on how to be healthier?

Well, in this book, you'll find a good companion.

Yes, there are always going to be challenges in life, but there are always ways through these challenges. And – with the final questions I give you in this book, and with a new perspective – everything can be easier,

SIGNED: A NORMAL SINGLE MOM

and a lot more enjoyable.

By the way, for privacy reasons, I will not refer to specific names; just know that I have four amazing kids, and that it was an absolute honour to raise them all.

As you read this, I am wondering who you are, my lovely reader. Maybe a daughter, a husband, a lover, a grandma, or a single mom. Who knows? Maybe you're a mom from China, Africa, or India. Or perhaps you're the happiest wife? If so, I wish you could tell me the secret – because I'm still not sure I understand it!

But whoever you are, I hope that you arrive at the end of this book with a smile, or a new view about something, or perhaps some relief or some renewed hope.

I wish all of these things for you and, most of all, I hope it helps you to appreciate – even more – what you already have.

SIGNED: A NORMAL SINGLE MOM

SIGNED: A NORMAL SINGLE MOM

CHAPTER TWO

WHAT DO YOU MEAN…NORMAL?

Although I don't have a favourite genre of music to have long, in-depth discussions about, I do harbour a love for music in general and enjoy countless artists.

I just joined a samba bateria band, even though the last time I played percussion instruments was 40 years ago. It's a lovely group of people of all ages, playing uplifting percussion instruments and shakers. You know that vibe where you just cannot stay still?!

Can you imagine the emotions I was feeling at the first trial lesson? When we were rehearsing, the joy, the fulfilment of creating an effect, the excitement of hearing so many different sounds becoming one, the pure energy pervading the whole church… it was really incredible.

SIGNED: A NORMAL SINGLE MOM

It was a good mixture of 'After all these years, I can still do it', and 'Let's see what I can learn now', with a little bit of 'Wow, how much energy can we create all together?!' mixed with a simple 'Why not?'

I signed up right away. It allows me to meet extraordinary people with all kinds of life experiences, and it's such a lovely moment to look forward to during the week.

Oh, and in case you want to bring some beat and vibes into your life, join us in Brighton! We are the Drum and Blaze.

I also love to dance, and after watching *Elvis* (twice), I got crazy about Elvis Presley, his songs, and – most of all – how the man could freaking dance. I immediately created a new playlist called 'Elvis' and, if I have him in my earphones, I simply cannot keep my legs still! Living in those days must have been such a blast.

I don't always shop at the same supermarket. I like nice and possibly cheap places, where the products are good, and where I like the vibe of the store. I like it if the store assistants are kind, efficient, or even

SIGNED: A NORMAL SINGLE MOM

funny, and are not annoyed if I ask, "How is your day?"

I have an amazing time at the grocery store on my road; we always have such friendly chats and hugs – plus a free fresh ready-to-eat fruit now and then, given with a smile.

Sure, I have a take-away now and then. Or some lovely café time with my kids, where we can chill and talk about things that didn't come up at home.

I always answer "Yes" when they ask me "Are you OK, Mom?" Once, my sweet daughter caught me with a tear in my eye, and she said: "Please Mom, let it out – you don't always have to look happy."

Yes, bless her – and me for having her!

I love cosy fancy socks, but I also love walking around the house barefoot, feeling the smooth warm wood or the fresh tiles beneath my toes.

I/we decorated our home as OUR home, our love nest, where everyone chose their own meaningful objects – rather than a stereotypical interior design magazine house where you feel like a stranger in your own home and where you feel afraid to touch anything. After all, who do you need to show it off to?

SIGNED: A NORMAL SINGLE MOM

I eat when I'm hungry. I am mainly vegan, but if I need that bigger boost, I have a couple of eggs with my avocado – and, man, I feel so good. So, call me as you like.

I absolutely love to blend an avocado, the perfectly ripen one, with oat milk. A kinda of baby food for me, delicious and filling.

I like to go to Primark especially in the winter season, and wander around the pyjama section. They always have the cosiest, fluffiest pyjamas, the ones you can snuggle up in while lazing around your house – and you know the price is going to be good too.

Whenever I want to buy a new mug, I don't know which old one to get rid of. They're all so full of memories, so I just end up adding another one to the collection. Do you also have a favourite mug for each mood and each drink? It's an important part of our morning, afternoon, and evening, isn't it?

I talk to strangers. Strangers are just people like you, with similar problems and joys as yours, but to whom you haven't talked yet. You can find so many funny, kind, and interesting people out there – maybe even future friends.

I feel like shit when the alarm goes off early in the morning during the school term, and I walk my first steps looking like an old woman. My son once told me that my morning yawns sound like a dinosaur. Fortunately, I start to feel awake quite quickly – but not thanks to coffee, which must wait until after I've had my early morning herbal spiced tea. So delicious and healthy.

I enjoy sleeping. I know, I know – now you're probably thinking I'm lazy, and that it's not what your mom taught you when she opened your bedroom door in the morning, always saying the same thing: "What? Are you still sleeping?!" when perhaps it was only 9am on a non-school day.

What I mean is that, to me, rest is sacred. It's the best way to recharge my body so that I'm in the best possible shape for anything I must deal with during the day. I like to perform my best, in any job I do. And I sleep so well.

Ever since they were little, I've let my kids wear what they want. I hate being forced to look like someone else wants me to look; it makes me feel uncomfortable. So why should I do this to my kids?

I remember my primary school years: every Sunday night, I was given a set of clothes that I was supposed to wear throughout the following week (bless my mom, I love her so much). I was always told what to wear, and I didn't particularly like it.

I love to go to the cinema, even by myself. After all, why shouldn't you go by yourself? There's no rule against it. And don't tell me you're worried about 'what other people think about you', because that should not be any of your business. They should be worried about what *I* think about *them* – just joking!

Besides, going to the cinema by yourself has some definite plus points: you don't have to share the popcorn, you can fully focus on the screen, the story, and the actors, and you can avoid back, neck and arm pain from bending on one side for two hours straight.

I love action, fantasy, and romance movies. Dreaming costs nothing. I loved going through all *Stranger Things* seasons with my kid; we made it our priority whenever a new season was released.

SIGNED: A NORMAL SINGLE MOM

My kids know I get excited about those little things, and sometimes they make fun of me because of it. Even so, I will continue showing them my enthusiasm and creating a nice positive contrast with those gloomy, depressed faces they might run into on social media.

Once, my kid told me I was weird, and I took it as a compliment.

One of the more 'normal' things I've done over the years is to try many different diets… did you do the same? I am always looking for what's best for my own body – and learning how to listen to it.

I haven't eaten meat or dairy in a long time. I was even a fruitarian for a bit; I felt light and glowing, so much energy…but something was missing. After doing keto for a while, I needed some unclog. Then I found out about the Blood Type Diet, and my body started asking me what the hell I was giving it. Then I went back to mainly juicy and delicious fruits, which are my number one thing, along with smoothies, vegetables, and warming soups.

I love intermittent fasting, which allows my

SIGNED: A NORMAL SINGLE MOM

body to rest and regenerate a bit every day.

What is that thing that is so normal but so special for You? I wish I could hear your answer.

I love my kids' gratitude, which is not for material things or expensive gifts, but from the heart – the true meaning of gratitude.

I am just a normal single mom, who tries not to forget to use her magic wand every day.

SIGNED: A NORMAL SINGLE MOM

CHAPTER THREE

I AM TRYING

I remember the first time I heard the word 'mindfulness' some years ago. I was wondering how I could be truly present in the moment – seeing the whole freaking universe in that sour apple – while I was looking for another part-time job. It was also parents' evening at school the following day, and I needed 'the father's signature' to fill out some useless forms. And, on top of this, my children wanted the latest Nintendo!

Seriously, I could see the flames in that apple... and I had plenty of directions where I could throw it.

How could I go for a walk with that old giggling schoolmate, who only ever talked about all the clubs she took her daughter to, while I showed sincere interest, and hid...oops... sorrow for the young daughter?!

How could I sit still in a meditation class, when

as soon as I closed my eyes, I could only see bills and upsets? Have you ever experienced this?

Those were certainly hard times.

Only you know how to show a smile to your kids – under any circumstances – with your unstoppable purpose to make them feel safe and OK.

I am so proud that my kids are my number one priority. How could they not be?! How can you not understand that they need your help, support, presence, love, and food, every single day of? Not on a weekly or monthly basis, but every single day – always.

Some things cannot be understood, so I stopped trying to understand them.

But I knew there had to be a way.

My favourite type of therapy has always been to just watch my kids. Whatever they were doing or saying, they always brought me back to life – to the reason why I had to make things go right. It made me want to find ways and ideas to make sure everything fell into place, no matter what.

They empowered me, as much as I empowered them.

SIGNED: A NORMAL SINGLE MOM

So, I persisted.

SIGNED: A NORMAL SINGLE MOM

CHAPTER FOUR

LET'S LEARN

For years now, I've not spent a day without learning something new or reading about something I was interested in – and I'm not talking about science texts or complicated matters.

It can be anything.

And I can assure you, I have a wide range of things I'm interested in or curious about, with those interests sometimes changing from one day to another. I just want to know what it's all about!

I am always surprised by how many different opinions there are about things online – often completely contradictory. You can find out that bananas are 'an absolute no-no if you want to lose weight', but also 'extremely helpful if you want to lose weight'… and the list goes on.

Has anyone ever told you that you're a nerd just

because you want to know or read something? Or that there is nothing more to learn? Or that you are too old to learn, so it's better to just sit on the couch and watch the news?

Well, I think life itself is a continuous learning process. Who knows what you – or even your kids – might need or find useful tomorrow? What if you find out about a new fascinating place to visit with them, a new way to stay healthy, or information about a passion you'd never thought of before? Or what if you searched online and understood something today that you never understood in history or geography years ago? Or... we could go on and on.

What if you, today, could take up a new sport, or cultivate a passion you couldn't afford when you were a child, or that you were stopped from doing? How would it make you feel?

I attended a fantastic online workshop about writing a book, and now here I am, writing a book for you, waking up in the middle of the night to jot down notes and ideas.

My kids are so proud. They've always been

amazing life advisers, regardless of their age. You can go and speak to them about any issue and, in return, you'll be given the most clean, simple, wise, sincere, effortless advice you could ever get.

I am so thankful. I have never treated them as 'ouchy-bouchy babies', but as amazing beings in little bodies.

"You are too little" or "You are this and that" have never been in my vocabulary, and now here they are: self-confident, respectful, independent, and kind.

Again, due to my curiosity and research, I thank God that none of them have ever been vaccinated, and they've always been so healthy – I can count on my fingers the number of school days they've missed over the years.

My kids once told me they never got bored with me because I always had a place to take them to. So true.

SIGNED: A NORMAL SINGLE MOM

SIGNED: A NORMAL SINGLE MOM

CHAPTER FIVE

MY PHYSICAL CONDITION

Ten years ago, after moving to the UK and going through a drastic lifestyle change – from a very active to a very sedentary one, from running every day to sitting at the computer eight hours a day, five days a week – my metabolism crashed.

This is true because it is true for me, not because of a doctor's explanation.

I felt like a Ferrari that had crashed into a wall. I started to look pale and weak, feeling sleepy every day after 2pm, and being ready to go to sleep every night at 7pm after getting home from work.

Can you imagine, as a mom, going home and finding your kids so excited to see you, ready for another intense and demanding evening, longing for all the attention they deserved... and you just dreaming about your bed? That's what it was like for me.

SIGNED: A NORMAL SINGLE MOM

It was an absurd form of fatigue that impeded me from being and doing everything I used to do when I was so fast and so full of energy. I no longer felt efficient enough for my kids or myself. I couldn't recognize myself. It was just so frustrating.

I remember crying once just because I was so tired, just like a child. Crying for your own tiredness! It was just such an unbelievable rejection of that unwanted feeling.

First, I wondered if alternative medicine could help me, since I'm not interested in medicines and drugs. I saw a little improvement, but it didn't last long.

I realised I needed a blood test. And, when I went to get the results at my local doctor's surgery, the GP – looking both concerned and angry – asked me immediately, "Don't you feel like shit??" (This part is not 'inspired by life events' – it's seriously what happened!)

I will never forget those words. I really hope that your GP is kinder and has a better bedside manner than mine had in those hard times.

She said I had 'hypothyroidism', which is when

your thyroid gland doesn't produce enough hormones and your metabolism slows down – which included all the symptoms I was experiencing. Another symptom is being highly sensitive to the cold – and, as many of my colleagues know, when I was cold, I was *super* cold.

Basically, the doctor told me I had to start taking a daily hormone tablet right away, and that I would have to keep taking it, every day, for the rest of my life. Well, that sounded serious – especially for someone who only took vitamins and supplements for everything – but I knew I had to start.

As I fast-forward to the present moment, I can tell you that I recently underwent a complete physical check-up, and the doctor delivered excellent news that all my vital indicators align with those of a 19-year-old.

I've lost weight since I moved to the sea with my kids – having been doing yoga almost every day and walking a lot – and I have plenty of energy to do what I need to do… if I don't go to sleep too late.

Over the years, I've done a lot of work with natural remedies and supplements, but I never stopped taking my daily hormone, which was life-changing for

SIGNED: A NORMAL SINGLE MOM

me.

I wish I could go back to that GP and proudly say, "I don't feel like shit anymore!" and thank her for her care, but I don't live there anymore.

I still remember the first night – after years of going to bed early – when I was still awake at 10pm with my kid, watching a movie... I couldn't believe it; I was so happy.

I don't know if you can relate to anything I said, but if you have any health issue regarding your own wellbeing, take care of it – without thinking that something else is more important (like we tend to do). Give it the proper time and attention it deserves. How can we do the job, otherwise?

Sometimes, when we feel sick, we also wonder how we could ever get back to how we were before. In that moment, it seems impossible... but nothing stays the same, and – with some good support and care – you can come back even stronger than before.

CHAPTER SIX

EHI, I'VE GOT REMEDIES!

Going back to when I was feeling like shit and had just started my daily hormone therapy, one of the first things I did was to find a job that would put me back in touch with people –in a physical manner, in 'real life' – like I had before. And, preferably, a job that was immersed in nature.

When I first found this place and felt the warmth of the people there, I fell in love. I knew straight away that it was where I wanted to be.

It was the welcoming biodynamic Table Hurst Farm in Forest Row – a cute and unique village in Ashdown Forest, in the southeast of England: a magical world all on its own.

I started working there as a barista, even though I had no experience (and, if you know me by now, you can probably guess that I searched online for how to make those amazing lattes even before I started!) and found the most amazing, loving, and welcoming people to work with.

Working there, I started to have a healthy, balanced life. I got moving again, and one of my kids loved to come and visit Mommy while she was working. He could enjoy the farm and the animals, as well as having babycinos– made with love by Mom.

I remember him telling me once, from the bottom of his heart, that he preferred to have no money at the end of the month, rather than me having to work two jobs. Another melting moment.

I never stayed without a job, but those words made me understand what kids really need.

I've found out that any job you do – if done responsibly, in the best way you can, while being kind and having a good purpose – is worth doing and is important… regardless of the label, or whatever it's called.

As a single mom, nothing is more important to me than keeping my job balanced with my family time, and with my own health and happiness. Who cares

SIGNED: A NORMAL SINGLE MOM

about a mom you never see, and who, when she comes home, is so exhausted you can't even talk to? Or how about someone who's never there to enjoy all the money she's been working so hard for?

I don't want to get to the end of my life and not be able to remember what I was doing with my kids for all those years, because I was just working all the time.

Well, after taking the daily hormone for a while, I started to feel better, and I had more colour in my face.

I did a lot of research, and I came up with a combination of supplements that I've taken daily ever since, which really helped me to recover. Consider that people often think I'm ten years younger than I am, and that when I go around with my eldest daughter, most people think I'm her sister or her friend. We laugh about it all the time.

I'm not saying this to show off. I just want to give you something to think about – and, who knows, it might be helpful for someone.

I don't know what your purpose is, but

regarding my body, my purpose is to have a healthy, long-lasting one that I can rely on to pursue all the things I want to do, travel and help all the people I want to help. It feels so good, and it makes my kids feel proud of me too.

For years, every morning I've had my cup of warm water with lemon, ginger, cinnamon, turmeric, and honey. Sometimes I alternate it with neem and turmeric in warm water.

As I said, I don't want this book to be a 'how-to' guide, so if you're curious, just do a little research online on the properties of these amazing herbs and spices. Powerful stuff.

Then, after around half an hour, I have my bulletproof coffee with coconut oil (blend your black organic Americano with it – it's sooo amazing and filling, but most of all, it has many health benefits. Give it a search).

During the day, I have coffee with oat milk, or herbal teas. And I'm still working on drinking enough water – just like everyone else!

The daily vitamins I take include A, B, C, D, E,

SIGNED: A NORMAL SINGLE MOM

Omega 3, sea kelp or spirulina, magnesium, calcium, potassium, and zinc. I also take Reishi mushroom tincture and Rhodiola Rosea. Again, it's interesting to know what these types of vitamins and supplements can do for you.

My enjoyable night's sleep is accompanied by the amazing properties of a spoon of ashwagandha in my nightly herbal tea. I was surprised when I read about all the benefits of this root (and yes, sure, why shouldn't they also list the side effects??). It helps me have a more relaxed sleep.

I've been taking collagen powder every evening for the last five years and I'm sure it has contributed to my healthy skin.

I don't like alcohol; it feels like poison to my body. Never liked smoking.

P.S. A gentle reminder: I am not a doctor. I'm just a normal single mom.

Secrets revealed.

SIGNED: A NORMAL SINGLE MOM

CHAPTER SEVEN

LET'S STAY HEALTHY

I am fully responsible for my own health. Nobody around here is taking me to the doctor or giving me sympathy if I have any aches or pains (thank God), and there's nobody around me who could potentially make me feel sick.

Why are you overeating… just because of someone else or the things they've done to you?

Why do you keep perpetuating that negativity by damaging your own health?

I am not a masochist. I love life – it is such a gift full of colours, beauty, magic, opportunities, good people, love, and dreams that can come true.

Seriously… if you suddenly got up and chuck your cookies, your alcohol, and all the rest in the bin… well done, I am so proud of you. It's just not worth it, and you are now one step closer to your freedom, to

SIGNED: A NORMAL SINGLE MOM

what you're worth, and to who you REALLY are.

I wish I could be there to jump around and laugh with you and go out for a walk – and why not? Make fun together of those old times when we were crying like babies.

CHAPTER EIGHT

A POEM TO MY KIDS

I've written poems and short stories ever since I was a kid. When I was nine, I got so excited to put together my first rhyme– a description of the sun! What an accomplishment. It is actually published at the end of my first book.

Do you like writing?

The first personal diary I had was given to me by my parents – for my birthday – when I was around that age. It had an image of the sea and some seagulls on each page, and it's such a precious object to me that I've always kept it. I also wrote in many diaries after that one.

Years ago, when I was living in Italy, I published a book of all the poems and short stories I'd written over the past 20 years. The translation of the title is: *To You: From Infinity*. When I read those pages,

SIGNED: A NORMAL SINGLE MOM

I wonder whether it was me who actually wrote them, because they're so beautiful (I know, I should stop minimizing myself; I'm still working on it).

The book even contains a poem-like letter, written to my not-yet-born kid, when I still didn't even have a partner. That is how much I wanted to be a mom in this lifetime.

My mom told me that, when I was a little girl playing with my new-born-looking doll, I would literally cry because the doll wasn't real! I don't remember this, but I trust my mom – and, besides, I can believe it.

What I remember well is that, at the age of 18, I had a boyfriend whom I'd loved for quite a while. Even at that young age, I had a clear dream of getting married and staying happily with him till the end of time. It just felt so effortless and normal. To me, it felt like the way things should naturally go.

I'm not sure what happened to that dream, but I guess something got in the way.

By the way, this is the poem I wrote to my four kids some years ago. I will try to translate it for you and

SIGNED: A NORMAL SINGLE MOM

hopefully make it sound as pleasant as it sounds in Italian:

TO MY KIDS

Joy that warms up my heart,
Life enlightening my own,
Free spirits I have guided along,
And towards freedom led.
The purpose of my work,
And my first thought of every day.

I, responsible for your coming,
Am forever honoured to have you by my side.

My aim was to show a smile in front of every shadow,
The aim is mine to never make you feel alone,
But instead fill up your heart with certainties and love.

Infinite love you gave me,
From the very first day I hugged you.

SIGNED: A NORMAL SINGLE MOM

I ask for forgiveness if I lacked any attention,
Or any reassurance,
But I promise I tried to do my best,
And the only exchange I've ever asked for was your happiness.

Infinite stars warming my path,
For whom I will always be there.

Mamma Simo x

CHAPTER NINE

NO PLANS TODAY

This morning, I am sitting here with my favourite mug, without a plan. There's a beautiful sun above the sea, and I love this smooth, chilled autumn that never really arrives.

On my favourite mug are the words: *'I Can't Keep Calm, My Son Is Getting Married'*.

I cannot believe that three years have gone by since their wedding day. They're such an amazing couple; they're so loving toward one another; it always looks like it's their first day together.

We often exchange love gifs in messages, without any words, because I think that love messages are superior to anything else– and the most meaningful messages don't even need words.

An unexpected heart or similar symbol showing up on your phone can mean so much: I Love

SIGNED: A NORMAL SINGLE MOM

You; I Am Here for You; I'm Thinking About You; We Are Close; You Are Not Alone…or Don't Worry – You Can Make It.

Do you also wish you could go back into the past, to when they were little, even just for 24 hours? I do.

As I write this, one kid is at school, another one is at her boyfriend's house, getting ready to start a new career soon, and my boys are happily busy with their lives.

Spending time together, like we used to do in the past, is sacred.

Just being around them –pretending to be busy while I listen to them talk to each other– is priceless to me. Do you also do that?

Family strength and union are so powerful and empowering.

I like this quote: "I have My Family. What is your Superpower?"

I think this was a good chapter… even without a plan.

SIGNED: A NORMAL SINGLE MOM

CHAPTER TEN

MY HAMSTER

Yes, when I say 'my', that's exactly what I mean. Mine. Like the one I had when I was ten years old.

Over the past few years, I've become tired of taking care of my kids' hamsters and pets, so – a few months ago – I bought myself my own hamster.

OMG, she's so cute. She was quite little but now she's grown up. She's super soft and light when you hold her, with white and ginger-colored fur and unique grey tips on her ears. She's not afraid of me at all; she's a well-mannered lady who keeps her cage tidy and uses different places to do different things. I've never seen anything like it.

You know she's my hamster because she does things differently: she often spins the wheel, but not in the usual way. She lies under it on her back and spins it fast using her paws!

SIGNED: A NORMAL SINGLE MOM

A few days ago, she did something that resulted in my living room having a new, fresh, cosier look.

Whenever something negative happens to you, you always try to turn it into something useful you can learn from, right?

Well, she escaped from a hole she'd chewed in her cage. I suppose she's just like any of us in the family: respectful at home, but ready to go out and explore the world at any time.

I searched everywhere for her, with the idea that the only place she was supposed to live was in her cage. Then I became more open-minded.

Once I'd made any electric wires unreachable, I let her do her thing around the house, while I was doing mine. After all, I knew she must be around somewhere, having fun.

Then an image came to my mind, of her trapped in some corner of our house, maybe full of escrements…so I started looking for her again.

And then there she was, sticking out from under the sofa – so cute! I tried to get creative, using tricks to get her out, but with no luck. She was so fast, darting back and forth under the sofa. I almost felt offended when she didn't want to jump into my hand – after all the good times we'd spent together!

Well, in the end, I had to start moving things around: the carpet, the sofa, the African drum... and then, suddenly, I had the idea to move all of the furniture around to give my living room a new look!

I finally grabbed Enola (fighter for freedom – that's why I called her that), settled her in a basket with her fluffy cotton and food, washed her cage, gave her fresh food and water, put a big stone from the beach in front of the cage hole, and then – when I finally went to place her back in her home, I found her completely asleep at the bottom of the basket, probably exhausted after the amazing adventure she'd had. Exhausted but surely happy.

Then, once I'd moved her back into her cage, it was time to create my new living room.

I won't go through everything, but I can tell you that I was surprised by my strength.

I got rid of things. I moved plants around. I moved everything else around too. Now my sofa is

SIGNED: A NORMAL SINGLE MOM

facing the big window and, when you're sitting there, looking at the sky, it feels like you're at the cinema. Everything is more open now, more in harmony, and it's even more pleasant to be there. My kids totally agree.

So, thank you, my sweet Enola.

A few days later, she won herself a brand-new cage, which was the best and fanciest one I'd ever bought. She deserved it.

And how are you getting on with your pets?

CHAPTER ELEVEN

A FUNNY QUOTE

I like quotes.

Does it ever happen to you, that when you read a quote, you wonder: *How the hell can this person define – with such perfect words and such a specific concept – what I've always thought, but have never found the words for?*

One night, after being inspired by my daughter's suggestion, I wrote around a hundred quotes just thinking about moments of someone's life. I was connecting to a specific moment, and magically words were coming out. So fascinating. I hope that one day you will see them all printed on amazing cards. Or maybe in a fantastic Quote Book.

I like quotes that make sense to me. Like this one I found on Facebook. It was something like:

'Women are like fruits. They are beautiful, juicy, colourful, and unique. The problem is men. They like fruit

SIGNED: A NORMAL SINGLE MOM

salads.'

What do you think about this one?

Sometimes I wonder if some men would like their child to have a husband like them. Yes, a very hot question.

CHAPTER TWELVE

A NICE PLACE TO BE

I realised that the only times I was successful with my kids were the times when I've been their friend.

Times when I was not judgmental, when I was not The Mom, but a listener – accepting what was shyly offered to me.

What followed were sincere hugs, a smile back on their face, more cuddles later, and – most importantly – trust.

I tried to offer a safe space where things could be said and acknowledged. Sometimes I failed big time. But then I tried to improve more and more.

And I find it amazing the way moms and kids can't help but forgive each other.

Some nights ago I went to the cinema, and the mom in the movie was showing regret and upset towards her grown-up daughter, ranting at her. In response, the daughter looked her in the eyes and replied, "Mom!"

They just looked at each other, and – in that moment – there was so much love and understanding, without any further words needing to be spoken, that I just cried.

I understood that, in a second, any regret was dissipated – because, in that bond, the only thing and the only strength that counts is mutual eternal love. Everything else is just drama.

Do you also think that life is a continuous journey where, every day, we find something to make it better and smoother? Because I do.

This pleasant September sun is really shining out there. I'm going to go and let him warm me up.

CHAPTER THIRTEEN

THE GUY (NOT 'THE GAY')

Some days ago, I was in a store – and man, one guy completely made me lose my mind.

My first thought was, *calm down, you know it would only lead to trouble. You can't just go to your kids one day and say, "Hi guys, this is my new partner, who you'll be seeing a lot of around the house…"*

I could already see their hopeless faces, and the family balance… unbalanced.

But I tell you, his simple inner and physical beauty was so intriguing to me.

I started to think the same things some people think around me: that I should find someone to share the rest of my life with, to help with supporting the kids… otherwise, I'll look selfish (have you ever had this one? I have). And that it's not OK that I want to do everything by myself and never accept any help.

SIGNED: A NORMAL SINGLE MOM

Then I thought about the people telling me I should not be afraid of the past, that they are not all the same, and that it is human nature that a woman must live with a man.

There are even people who have told me to keep a man just to guarantee financial security. We all have different values, right?

Then I started to think of the other 50% of the people, telling me not to make the same mistake, and that my kids' relationship with him would never work, and that I would give myself a bad image, being with another man.

And while the angels were fighting against the demons in my head, the guy in the store kept on hanging around me, in that cosy blue hoodie, looking for some fancy tea boxes right next to me (and if I'm honest, I liked to think he was pretending to do that… just to be near me).

Then I thought again that what people think about me is none of my business.

Great – I instantly felt lighter and a lot better. I should have just followed my heart and my instinct.

SIGNED: A NORMAL SINGLE MOM

What would you have done?

Then, a cool guy appeared from behind the aisle and walked towards him, looking at him with a sweet smile – which was instantly returned.

Shit, he was gay.

Sorted.

SIGNED: A NORMAL SINGLE MOM

CHAPTER FOURTEEN

GO TO YOUR DEATH BED ONE SEC, NOT JOKING

A few months ago, a series of fortunate events changed my life (and you know that, if my life changes, my kids' lives do too).

I started to read an amazing book called *The Enchanted Life* by Sharon Blackie – which had simply stood out from the library shelf, telling me, "Hey, I'm here!"

It showed me that an Enchanted Life has to do with falling in love with the world all over again.

I completely fell in love with that concept. I had to read that description over and over because the more I read it, the deeper it reached my heart.

I started to remember how exciting everything had been when I was a child – and when I say everything, I mean *everything*, from the smallest and most common things around me to the biggest and more visible ones.

How magical my world was – or how magical I could make it – when I was spending my time alone, playing by myself. I could also play-act with my cousin for hours, getting so much into the scene that I would find myself literally crying! And let's not talk about walking in the woods or playing in my grandma's garden…I love you Nonna, you are the sweetest person I have ever met (yes, I wrote an amazing poem for her as well, which is like a portrait of her in words).

Then I watched a couple of movies about the lives of famous artists. The common denominator? They just did not give a f**k about what others – including the authorities – were saying; they just pushed forwards, towards what they believed in, and they succeeded (apart from taking drugs – a big trap).

Then I did something: I drew a map of my life from the beginning, noting down all the main events and paying particular attention to when I had dreams and when I didn't. This chart started to become very interesting indeed.

And then, there I was: I arrived at the present day. I thought it was the end of my exercise. It was the end of the chart. So… now what?

Well, a brand-new view opened before me. I decided to continue drawing the line – making it as long as the one I'd just filled up with events, emotions, dreams, and facts – and there it was: the second half of my life, completely blank, waiting to be filled up, created, and designed. And man, it was so long!

In that moment, I felt like I was being reborn.

My fifty-one years represented – as well as being mathematically true –the start of the second part of my life. All the feelings I had around dredging things up from the past, and the habits of doing the same thing just because you've always done it, so you must continue it, or the feeling that you will not have any other chance, or that it's too late, or that you must adjust to life because you're not young anymore… all those burdens just disappeared.

Right there in front of me, I saw a beautiful vast white canvas that was just waiting to be painted.

How would you feel if you were given one

more brand-new chance?

Days before I told one of my kids that I used to dream of becoming an actor, and that if I had the chance to go back to when I was a child, I would have attended drama school from the beginning. I did some acting in commercials years ago, but then I stopped.

He calmly replied, with the simplicity with which kids see life, "Do it now."

Those words reached my heart in such a true, trustworthy way that they could not have sounded truer to me. In that moment, I felt completely lit up. My kiddo was so right.

I think that our life belongs to us. And that our destiny depends on nobody else but us. After all, who else is it up to?!

The neighbors who look at you every day, gossiping and making sure you continue to do the same things over and over?

Or your parents, who wanted you to do something that was not You?

Or your 'friends', so that you can continue to please them?

SIGNED: A NORMAL SINGLE MOM

Or some kind of laziness or self-pity, which pushes you down and makes you waste your life?

Or maybe what your teacher or family used to say, that 'you are not good enough'?

In my mind, I went into the future – to me lying on my deathbed – and I looked down at my life.

If I were to do that, what would I see?

I would have seen a lifetime of jobs done here and there, just to carry on, just to make money, just because I was a mamma, just to wait until I got older… and that's it.

And down there, way back… that amazing dream I had of becoming an actor was just sitting there. A dream I could have accomplished and enjoyed with all the ability, potential, and passion I had.

How the hell would I have felt??? What a wasted life! I would have felt so sad and angry at myself because it would have been too late to go back. Too late even to let my kids have a more enjoyable and more fun mom throughout their life, a mom who'd gone after what she really wanted to do.

That scenario was enough to make me jump

back to that unforgettable evening in July 2022. I decided, saw, and felt – with every fibre of my being – that, from now on, I would start acting classes and live as an artist. I would start to follow that path, no matter what, along with everything else.

I started to feel so much myself that, suddenly, everything made sense – what I've always done, how I've always felt. Like an artist.

My body started to feel differently, and I wanted to move and dance. I started to think in a different way, and see things in a different way, from the point of view and with the eyes of an actor and artist.

I couldn't sleep that night, and for at least ten nights after that.

That very night, in the moonlight, I searched online and found a drama school in my town where I could take acting classes.

The day after was one of the most enjoyable days I've ever had. My kid and I went on a trip to a coastal town, and we kept finding magic in all the places we went, and in all the things we did.

SIGNED: A NORMAL SINGLE MOM

But the magic was in me, casting everything in a completely different light. I was feeling exactly like myself, no matter what I'd been supposed to do – or who I was supposed to be.

After that, life with my kids became even more enjoyable and much more fun, because I could be with them and experience the imagination and creativity of a child. It also became much easier to find things to do – and things to say.

Well, from that day onwards, the most exciting and juicy part of my life started. I began taking acting classes, which I really recommend to you, even just to come out and free your natural self – and then go back home in a way you've never felt before. You can also meet so many amazing and friendly people.

I can now make my kids laugh more, and I had to inform my neighbours that if they heard me screaming, talking loudly, singing or dancing, not to worry – I've just gone back to art.

SIGNED: A NORMAL SINGLE MOM

CHAPTER FIFTEEN

WRITING A BOOK

I think that you should write a book.

The good news is that you don't have to be an expert.

I am sure there's something that only You can write about, and we would be so happy to hear and read all about it.

Matt Rudnitsky is the amazing author who inspired me to write again. I found his online workshop where he explains – in simple terms – how to write a fantastic book (I know I'm putting myself at risk now; I don't mean that my book will be fantastic… or maybe I do… but that's what Matt was inspiring us to do).

As I was listening to him, I was already writing down the title of my new book.

Matt completely got me when he talked about the purpose of a book: to help other people. To change someone's life. To make someone's life better. And that made me rush straight to my keyboard.

That's why I thought that you, lovely reader, might be ready to write your own book. Being You is Wisdom; nobody else has the same experiences you've had.

Competition only exists to minimise yourself. Nobody else can offer what You can offer. And this, of course, is valid throughout all areas of your beautiful life.

I believe we all have something to share. Something inspiring. Something in which we're not necessarily experts, but something we know enough about to make someone else not feel alone.

Writing a book means that you can talk to someone (or to many people all over the world) and make them really feel and understand something. You can make them see that they can go to the cinema by themselves, or that they can learn how to love someone so much that you just want to cry, and you feel your heart exploding. Or perhaps you went on an amazing trip that you'd like the whole world to know about, or perhaps your imagination just created such an amazing story that nobody else could ever conceive of it.

The other good news about writing a book is that there is no limit to how many books can be written or how many subjects can be talked about. I am sure there are thousands of stories that people still haven't told, thousands of titles still unrevealed, and thousands of things people would be interested to read about.

And, adding that magic to your life every day – where you sit with your cuppa and let it all come out – is priceless and life-changing, for others and for yourself.

Forget about being a good kid in school, writing a perfect essay to get a high score, and just be there yourself – with your life, your thoughts, what you want to share, and your wish to help someone.

If you were to write a book, what would you talk about? And what would you be afraid of?

Set yourself free of the fear of being judged, because you might get judged anyway later when you go out to do your shopping, right? But who cares? It's their problem.

SIGNED: A NORMAL SINGLE MOM

Be You. Do You.

Maybe I'm not helping you on the subject I write about in this book, but at least – since you're reading this – maybe I am helping you distract yourself from someone annoying around you…ha-ha!

I am sure that starting to write your own book will unravel abilities you didn't know you had.

And don't be surprised if, at the beginning, you find yourself waking up in the middle of the night and jotting down some notes that just came to mind!

Perhaps now it will be your kids' turn to shout at you, "Lights out!" late at night.

CHAPTER SIXTEEN

THIS PAGE IS ALL FOR YOU

START WRITING YOUR BOOK.
 I will be honored to receive it:

SIGNED: A NORMAL SINGLE MOM

SIGNED: A NORMAL SINGLE MOM

CHAPTER SEVENTEEN

I COULD CRY

I was just carrying on with my day as usual, when my son sat next to me and told me the most touching, most unexpected words I've ever received.

He said: "Mom, I would like to be like you. Because you are always happy, people like you, and you know how to speak to people."

That was a moment of priceless acknowledgement, where all the doubts I had – of whether I do enough or not –simply disappeared. Even the self-doubt that had been instilled in me when people said things like 'you aren't a good example' and stuff like that… it all just blew away in one second.

I felt so happy, flattered, recognised, and loved in that one second, I could cry.

I didn't know how to thank my son and, after feeling this glorious moment of self-accomplishment,

SIGNED: A NORMAL SINGLE MOM

I immediately realised my help was needed on the other side.

I will not go through the chat we had, or everything I went through with my son to make him feel happier and to achieve what he wanted – because, as I said at the beginning, I am not an expert nor a guide – but we surely got up from that sofa both feeling accomplished… and with a plan.

I also learnt that, sometimes, you believe that someone thinks of you in a certain way, but that assumption can be wrong – and it can be surprisingly different when you openly ask that person what they think of you, or they just tell you (I know this sentence is not professionally articulated, but I just wanted to say it as if I were talking to you in front of our coffee. I hope you like it too).

CHAPTER EIGHTEEN

PUMPKIN SPICE LATTE

As I'm writing this book, the beautiful, peaceful, sweet season of autumn has arrived.

The best quote I found today on Facebook is this: *'The trees are about to show us how lovely it is to let things go'* (by Unknown), with a lovely image of some red and yellow leaves lying quietly on a fresh damp pavement.

I am curious to see what autumn looks like by the sea – compared to where I was living before, in Ashdown Forest, where going to work in the morning always took me longer than it should because I always stopped to admire those amazing tall red and yellow trees along the way. What a magical view I got in that season!

What I love about living by the sea (well, one of the hundred things I love about it) is watching the colour of the sea every day, which is never the same.

SIGNED: A NORMAL SINGLE MOM

As well as the shape and flow of the waves – and the clouds.

Every day, every walk I do is different, and how the sky will join the ocean that day is always unpredictable.

A light rain can suddenly be followed by sunrays, a rainbow can appear so often, friendly people can be met at any time, and any day you can find a new cosy café to enjoy your coffee, to eat some food you've never tried before, or to find new connections that can change your life – either a lot or just a little bit.

I feel sorry for people who spend so much time worrying about the past, which has gone, or the future, which is not here yet and might be different from what we think. In these cases, you end up missing the amazing present moment, where your loved ones and all kinds of wonderful opportunities are, looking straight at you.

Autumn this year is coming very gently and seeing pumpkin spice lattes all around makes me want to have one.

This morning I've decided to make my own at

home, avoiding all those sugary fake ingredients (don't worry; I also enjoy them sometimes when I'm in town with a friend) – and why not? I'm saving some pounds.

I get half a cup of coffee, blend it with my oat milk, add some spices like cinnamon, ginger, and nutmeg, and sweeten it with some good honey – et voila! I then put it in a nice glass and top it with cinnamon powder. Delicious!

I can highly recommend this if you like these kinds of body-and-soul-warming hot drinks.

I'd love to know what your favourite hot drink is if you have one.

SIGNED: A NORMAL SINGLE MOM

CHAPTER NINETEEN

MY YOGA

My very first yoga session took place during full lockdown, in my bedroom, after I had COVID. My daughter had started some days before – in her bedroom, of course – and had suggested I try it because it was making her feel better.

So, I downloaded the 'Down Dog' app (which sounded like a weird name to me, until I found out it was the name of a yoga position), set up a few minutes to start with, and then followed the flow and the music.

I liked it, so I kept doing it, and even ordered my own yoga mat. I loved the beautiful soothing music, as well as the lovely girl performing the positions in such an effortless way – and in a variety of position combinations – every time. I started to love my appointments with her.

I must admit, it was one of the elements that

contributed to my recovery from COVID, getting my body going again.

Once recovered, I got back to my running, which has been my favourite sport ever since I was a little girl. But then I moved to the seaside, winter came, and – not being the best runner in the cold – I started to enjoy my living room more: a perfect scenario to lay down my yoga mat and keep practicing… without freezing!

Since then, I haven't stopped. My set minutes became longer, the choice of body parts to boost got wider, and my muscle flexibility began to change.

I started to feel lighter throughout the day, started to see how I could reach points I could have never dreamed of before. My balance got better, my posture got better, my body started to have a more defined shape, and I really enjoyed the feeling of relaxation I always got after just the first few minutes.

And what about the 'do it when you want' and 'wear what you want' side (even though I tend to do it at the same time every day and look pro for my self-esteem)?

SIGNED: A NORMAL SINGLE MOM

Well, as you know from the beginning of this book, I am not an expert, and I'm sure that – thinking about your super cool yoga lessons at the yoga center with yoga practitioners, and your spiritual yoga trips to the Far East – you're going to laugh at me. I wish you could teach me more.

But I thought about all the single moms at home with kids – and their time and money availability – and I thought that this might be inspiring for someone.

I also think that with self-discipline, so much can be accomplished.

SIGNED: A NORMAL SINGLE MOM

CHAPTER TWENTY

BEETROOT CRISPS PETITION

I think that they should put many more beetroot crisps in the root vegetables crisp packets.

I hope you agree with me.

As a matter of fact, my kid also says they should put more crisps in all bags of crisps.

Have you ever felt disappointed when opening one?

That's all I want to say today.

SIGNED: A NORMAL SINGLE MOM

SIGNED: A NORMAL SINGLE MOM

CHAPTER TWENTY-ONE

YES, OR NO?

Do you have more days when you think you should have a new partner, or more days when you think that your current state is perfect, and that you couldn't ask for more?

Are engaged women wishing to be single, or are single women jealous of engaged ladies?

And whatever your answer is, is it coming from your heart, or has it been dictated by what people think about you, and expect from you?

Can you see how the negative can be positive – if you want it to?

How could someone take advantage and benefit from an apparently unlucky situation?

Is it as bad as described?

Who wishes to be you?

Of course, I am not here to give you answers –

SIGNED: A NORMAL SINGLE MOM

just reflection points.

I think that the meaning of 'single' must come from someone's heart and reflection. Not a socially stereotyped label.

And, once it's found, I believe it should be carried with full responsibility and personal pride.

CHAPTER TWENTY-TWO

IT CAN ONLY HAPPEN IN BRIGHTON (I THINK)

It was a beautiful late summer Saturday morning in Brighton, and my daughter and I decided to spend some good girl time together – we went to the Lanes and got lost amongst the colours, faces, clothes, and fascinating objects you can only find in that area.

It is so nice to walk around there when you're not working, as if you were a tourist, knowing that you are so lucky to live close by.

Often, you end up buying something that stole your heart the last time you were there.

Well, it was time for my chai latte and some good food for my daughter.

Usually, it takes us a while to decide where to eat, because the choice of cute cosy cafés is so vast that

SIGNED: A NORMAL SINGLE MOM

we never know which one to try first.

But that day we decided to go and see some friends who were working in a unique café with a balcony overlooking the Lanes (by the way, it's called 'Kenny's Rock & Soul Café', if you ever go there – and enjoy the place where a special writer once sat).

It's just so nice to sit above that colourful buzzing street, embellished by the balcony's flowers, the sky, curious pigeons coming and going, and good music. And knowing I had no appointments that day… bliss!

We sat at a little table, had a chat with our lovely friends who served us, and then the food and drinks arrived. My chai latte was delightful, and the cinnamon on top was spicier than usual –great. While I enjoyed my drink, we had an interesting chat about my daughter's future travel plans and much, much more.

Meanwhile, a lovely lady sat next to us and started to enjoy her full English breakfast. As often happens in Brighton, you end up talking to everyone around you. She was kind enough to make a probably

SIGNED: A NORMAL SINGLE MOM

hungry pigeon fly away from us simply by gently waving her newspaper at it.

We exchanged some words, including where we all came from, and then she went back to her breakfast while we carried on with our chilled conversation.

And then there we were – looking at each other in a timeless moment, surprised and confused, bursting into the biggest laugh – when the lady said she thought… we were partners! OMG.

Welcome to Brighton.

SIGNED: A NORMAL SINGLE MOM

CHAPTER TWENTY-THREE

TO THE FATHERS WHO DO NOT FINANCIALLY SUPPORT THEIR KIDS, USING ANY PERSONAL JUSTIFICATION THEY CAN COME UP WITH, THINKING THAT MAYBE TODAY THEIR KIDS DON'T NEED ANY FOOD OR CLOTHES

SIGNED: A NORMAL SINGLE MOM

CHAPTER TWENTY-FOUR

I WANT IT CUT REALLY SHORT

It was full lockdown. Everything just felt so stuck – an unexpected stop to our usual, everyday lives that didn't seem to make any sense.

The new year was at the door, my 50th birthday was coming up, my kids and I were planning to move to the sea, and I needed to do something extraordinary to come out of the old and mark the start of a brand-new beginning.

My hair had been long, beautiful, and wavy for years. And I mean long– halfway down my back.

It was gorgeous, yes, but I was getting tired of receiving all the compliments and associations between 'me' and 'my hair'. Tired of the same old look.

I needed a new Me to represent the whole new life I was going to create.

SIGNED: A NORMAL SINGLE MOM

So, I decided to cut all my hair off – and I mean no middle ground at all. In a few minutes, it went from very long to very short, almost shaved.

Of course, how it got done during full lockdown will remain a mystery.

Boom. Done. And there I was. Almost shaved. Such a feeling of freedom, lightness, and simplicity – a total feeling of being myself.

If someone was going to like me now, it would have been for who I am. Not for my hair.

That was the gift I gave to myself on my 50th birthday. And I was happy to give a gift on that day to someone else, too.

I donated my long hair – nicely tied up – to a charity that creates wigs for kids who have lost their hair due to cancer.

I cannot think of the sadness and frustration a young girl or boy must feel, losing her or his hair.

Knowing that I would have created at least one smile through my hair donation was so touching. I wished I could have seen that smile, but of course, it wasn't possible.

SIGNED: A NORMAL SINGLE MOM

I just want to say that if you ever thought about having your hair cut short because you fancy it and because you want to feel free and comfy, and like yourself, but then you start thinking about what others would think, and you end up not doing it… stop that thinking right now. You should go and do it. For you.

Another contorted paragraph coming out of my heart.

You would then thank yourself for being so brave and for loving yourself, and you would realise that it is so true that what other people think about you is none of your business.

In fact, so many people asked me why I hadn't done it before and said I should have always had short hair!

But that, again, comes under 'what other people think about me' –and you know my thoughts on that.

I wish you could tell me the craziest or most meaningful thing you did during full lockdown, so that we could laugh over it.

SIGNED: A NORMAL SINGLE MOM

CHAPTER TWENTY-FIVE

THOUGHTS

Some women think that a man is a man because he pays stuff.

I think that the definition of a man must also include that he respects you, whether you are present or not.

And also that he uses his muscles and strength to carry shopping bags and to fix damned broken things around the house, rather than against a beautiful woman like you.

You cannot be replaced.

Be strong. Wish them no pain but to heal. Whatever happened, honestly accept it, learn something from it, use it to set great goals for the future, and then start pursuing them.

You made it. You can look into your kids' eyes every day and say, "I'm here, how can I help you? We

SIGNED: A NORMAL SINGLE MOM

are a team." You can ask them what they want and need from you, every day.

My reward has been amazing kids telling me, "If you're happy, Mom, we're happy" … or "Thank you Mom for making me the Man I am today."

Everything is going to be fine.

SIGNED: A NORMAL SINGLE MOM

CHAPTER TWENTY-SIX

THE LONELY MOMENTS

There's a recurring quote that I often see on social media and in the movies: *'Being alone does not mean being lonely.'*

Once you understand this, and personally experience it, you can be happy again.

Your 'lonely moments' are moments you can fill up with things you like to do.

Learn to do something, invest in your personal growth, help your neighbour, explore new places, or go out for your favourite coffee with your favourite book or your favourite friend.

And you will never hear me tell you to drink alcohol, which will just make your loneliness worse.

Walk through a crowd of people you don't know and enjoy looking around – maybe do some body language observation... a very interesting thing to

SIGNED: A NORMAL SINGLE MOM

do which I learnt at acting classes. You can notice so many fascinating attitudes that the body uses to express feelings, to get or give attention, and so on.

Local community centres are always friendly and inspiring places to explore. They often host interesting activities to take part in for very little money – or even for free – and one should never feel wrong for joining in.

Go out with other single parents.

Renew your wardrobe.

Change your style.

Take a restorative nap and have better perspectives after it.

Go out for a walk and see things you've never noticed before.

There is so much to explore and to know outside.

Find the history of your current town so that you feel even more 'at home'.

Buy new shoes – a fool proof method for Italian moms. You always need a new pair, some new different shoes 'you really needed', right? Absolutely my philosophy ahah! A philosophy that made me collect thirteen pairs of trainers of all colours I absolutely adore…and yes, I know that might not be under the category of 'normal', but I think that everyone should have her/his own personal collection of something, right? That's Simo's. What is yours?

You can make a phone call to someone you love. Not for gossiping, nor to speak badly about your ex – which would only make you feel worse and let the negativity persist. But just to have a good time and enjoy being connected.

Maybe there's even someone who needs help, and you know you could do it well.

Never be afraid to ask for help yourself.

What do you like doing? What passion do you nurture? What gives you joy?

The past cannot be changed; it's gone. The only thing we have is our present and future, so let's not miss this chance to do a great job now.

Maybe even an excellent one.

Start asking yourself, "Why Not?"

SIGNED: A NORMAL SINGLE MOM

CHAPTER TWENTY-SEVEN

MY MOM

I love my mom.

She has always been present, sometimes even in moments I was not expecting her to be. In good moments – like when she showed up at the airport on my first flight as a flight attendant – and in moments where I was in need… the less pleasant moments.

There is some kind of magical connection between us, where one of us perceives what the other is thinking, without speaking. Have you ever experienced that?

Our phone calls usually start with, 'I was just going to call you,' or, 'I was just thinking of you.'

She worked hard all her life, and only now do I really understand the way she behaved – the afternoon naps she took on the sofa, and all the effort she made not to make me feel like something was missing, despite all the difficulties. I never felt I couldn't have something I needed, and I still wonder now how she was able to do it.

As a kid, I always liked to exchange her love and everything she did for me with cuddles, writing messages and cards to her, doing chores, being kind, going shopping for her, and warming up her cold bedsheets before she went to bed in the evening – rubbing my little feet together in my pyjamas under her blanket. I always wanted to see her happy.

She was always supportive of the activities I did as a kid, trusting in my abilities– and always so proud of my school results.

We had an amazing time together where I grew up in Italy in her Fiat 500, with her driving it, and me standing up on my seat, holding myself in the open roof with my little face sticking out, and losing my hat so many times – either up in the mountains or along the lake where I was born.

I learnt from her how to make my kids feel my presence, either when I'm right next to them, or far away.

SIGNED: A NORMAL SINGLE MOM

If there is something I can bring to her right now, it is a safe space where she can feel happy and understood, and feel free to be herself.

She recently told me that my richness is my smile and my happiness – a totally unexpected compliment that went straight to my inner heart and made me cry. Not everyone knows you so well.

I replied that it's true: my happiness can be created at any moment during the day. It is within me, and it doesn't depend on a bank account, which is the reality she often sees around her.

Of course, she adores my kids, and they love their Nonna too, and I love that they write each other cards from different parts of the world.

What positive aspects of the life you have or had with your mom, did you bring with you, in raising your children? I would be so curious to know.

I think that, in all languages, there is nothing that can be compared to the sound of 'Mamma'. Try to say it out loud: it's a mixture of a soft blanket, a hot chocolate or warm milk with honey, your favourite cookies…and a big hug.

SIGNED: A NORMAL SINGLE MOM

Such a rich word, full of warmth, love and… everything.

Grazie, Mamma.

CHAPTER TWENTY-EIGHT

CHILD ANXIETY

I hear my kids talking more and more about their friends being affected by anxiety or depression, and even online it's becoming a recurring issue.

I remember people talking about this subject only on one occasion when I was a kid.

I think there were fewer triggers back then. Or less labelling.

Or fewer drugs.

Fewer unrealistic icons to follow and less comparison.

Maybe school was easier, less complicated.

Parents less overprotective?

Better and more simple food?

Only the television was available. Fewer horror movies.

More books to read and airplanes to build.

SIGNED: A NORMAL SINGLE MOM

And, indeed, more meetings in the courtyard and playing outside. My good old 80s.

I wonder if the anxiety percentage is higher in kids living with a lone parent who tries to do her/his best, or in kids living with continuously fighting and screaming or cheating parents, who keep it all together because they must.

The reasons must be endless and may have nothing to do with what I thought about before. I just wish – for every single kid on Earth who is suffering from it – the peace and the happiness they deserve… and were born to experience.

CHAPTER TWENTY-NINE

WHAT ELSE SHALL I WISH FOR?

Some days ago, I texted my son. He's such a lovely, kind, sweet, and hard-working being. (And yes, you all are, in case his brothers and sisters are reading this!).

I know what you are thinking, and I bet each single mom would use an infinite list of adjectives, when addressing to her own children… like I do. And they would all be true.

Anyway, I just wanted to let him know how proud I was of him for everything he takes care of, and for how he is. And, of course, how much I love him.

Why should you take feelings for granted? It is so nice to remind our family members and friends of our love. It might arrive as a shining star to brighten up their day.

His reply was a short text:

SIGNED: A NORMAL SINGLE MOM

'You did everything.' Another ray of sun through my heart.

How about another memory? It was Father's Day, and I opened the card that my daughter had kindly given me, to find, *'Thank you for being my father'* written inside.

Those are the moments when you realise that, yes, you are doing your best – and even more than you thought.

CHAPTER THIRTY

LET IT ALL GO

We are used to believe what we're told – especially in an emotionally stressful moment, when we feel weaker and more vulnerable than usual.

We accept others' opinions because we think that other people are better than us, that they know more than us and have more experience than us.

Then we carry on our lives with that belief, letting it become so much a part of us that we think it is Us, burying – and forgetting – where it came from.

These can be some of those ghosts:

You will starve without me.

I cannot leave you alone for one second or you will emotionally crash, and I must come and rescue you.

You cannot do anything without me.

You will not make it.

SIGNED: A NORMAL SINGLE MOM

How can you make so much money by yourself?

You start doing so many things and you always end up with nothing.

You cannot achieve your dreams anymore.

You are too old now.

Women at your age start having health issues.

You should slow down and think only about your kids.

You are not good enough.

How many of these can you relate to?

Well, ask yourself where these thoughts come from – every single one of them – and if they've ever served you. Are those beliefs helping your life?

Then, I want you to look around and see if you can find any fact to prove them: see where you're living, the smile of your kids, the activities they do, the love and gratitude they give you, the things you do together, your days out, the help you give to each other, the plans you have for tomorrow, how many adversities you overcame alone, how many times you made it, the last thing you bought to your kids and to yourself, the things you like to do, where you were before, and the progress you've made so far.

Make a list of all your accomplishments, studies, efforts, and the energy you've put into the things you have achieved. Then congratulate yourself and tell me if those beliefs are true.

Exactly – they're all rubbish. You can throw them all out the window.

Allow yourself to let them go.

Create your new beliefs, coming from Your heart and Your values. New personal beliefs you're going to change the world with – and which will bring you the success you've always wanted, deserved, and have always been able to achieve.

SIGNED: A NORMAL SINGLE MOM

CHAPTER THIRTY-ONE

WE SHOULD SPEAK MORE

Yes, that's what I think. We should speak more.

To the people around us who can listen without judgement.

To the people who should stop telling us what to do, because we'll never do it anyway – because it is Their solution and Their perspective, which is different from ours, due to our individual experiences.

But we should speak more. About anything.

So many accidents in people's lives could have been avoided, if only someone would have opened their heart to a person they could have – and should have – trusted.

We have a problem, but we think nobody would understand, so we don't speak about it to anyone. And then, caught by fear of the unknown, we make mistakes, and we get into trouble.

SIGNED: A NORMAL SINGLE MOM

If only we had taken a deep look around us and found a person that our heart felt safe with – if only we would have expressed our thoughts and emotions to them – then maybe the problem would have seemed easier to solve, and we wouldn't have taken those dangerous steps.

There are good people around us.

I know that life might have taught us not to trust anyone anymore, but the moment we break this belief, we might find relief on the other side – and a more pleasant and happier life.

Talking to someone who wants the best for you might give you creative ideas and solutions you've never thought about before.

You may get rid of barriers you had created yourself.

You can see how everything could be much worse.

It can make you feel that, in the end, you are lucky just to have 'that' problem, and you might feel grateful for all the things you already have.

We should speak more. We should get rid of all

SIGNED: A NORMAL SINGLE MOM

those negative thoughts and focus more on our strengths and our competence – and on our future and what we want to achieve.

In the end, we are not our thoughts.

So, making a little effort, who could you speak to today, and about what? How could it help you feel better and lighter?

Maybe today is the right day to do it.

We should speak more.

SIGNED: A NORMAL SINGLE MOM

SIGNED: A NORMAL SINGLE MOM

CHAPTER THIRTY-TWO

A YOGA PRINCIPLE

You Are Right Just as You Are.

Isn't it beautiful? Calming. Reassuring. True.

Isn't it something we've always known? We just need to be reminded of it.

I am sure that my kids see me in a different light than how I see myself. They often tell me to stop doing this or that because I'm OK just as I am.

We always tend to watch what other people do, look like, and have.

Even what other moms do! We think that maybe they are super organised, super disciplined, that their house is super tidy, their kids are super busy, and they look so cool that they must follow some special diets, and 'know about life definitely more than us'. And maybe they're lucky enough to have parents helping them financially.

SIGNED: A NORMAL SINGLE MOM

Now let's look at the reality: How many of those thoughts are true? Maybe they are so full of worries that they don't even see you passing by.

Why let others dictate how we're doing? Why not appreciate our beauty, the magic we create, and how we do it? Why not accept us for what we are and what we give to the world every day – and the love and uniqueness we infuse into it?

I would replace 'compare yourself to' with 'be inspired by'. It would surely be more useful in our lives.

What are the unique, special, and lovely qualities that make you as beautiful as YOU are?

We are loved for what we are, and I'm sure our kids wouldn't change us for anybody else in the entire world. Ok I am crying on this one.

SIGNED: A NORMAL SINGLE MOM

CHAPTER THIRTY-THREE

I JUST WANTED TO LET YOU KNOW

I must admit that between you and my children always win my children… unless they are in school!

I realized that I did what I did (and someone may wonder 'how?!') just because I love my kids, exactly like you. And that's 'how' you do it, every single day.

I prefer honesty over sympathy. I am quite self-confident and most of the times my choices and decisions have proved correct.

I really love you, but when you ask me to stay out late, I just cannot wait to go back home to see my kids. They're so much my priority that it cannot be explained. Don't take it personally.

I feel sad to hear that some married moms feel like single moms. At least they're still in a place where they can sort everything out, they can still sit down and talk and they are still in time to say what they want, what they miss, what they need, their yeses and their nos.

I am sure there are moments when we all wish we had a time machine to take us back to 'that' moment – so that maybe we could do something different.

Or back to any point. Maybe even well before that.

And then what?

Accept. Learn. Look ahead. Carry on.

I think that if it is positivity, a good heart and abundance what you radiate, that's what you get back.

I think that the universe is so full of possibilities and opportunities that can show up to you, if you just keep your heart open, and believe in everything that is already inside you.

Can you decide to change your life for the better, today, from any position and place you are right now?

SIGNED: A NORMAL SINGLE MOM

CHAPTER THIRTY-FOUR

I HEAR YOU

Everyone has a different journey.

A different reason and beginning, a different time to fix everything and to find a balance, where things can take off again and a more pleasant life can be lived and enjoyed.

Every single mom has a unique experience, and I want to acknowledge every single one of them for their strength, their courage, their resilience, and the hardships they've had to face.

I know that in any case, it has been an enforced, unwanted situation nobody planned and wished for. What a scary moment was the "How the hell am I going to make it?" one.

Well, the answer I've found is this: "You have to do it."

You can do it.

SIGNED: A NORMAL SINGLE MOM

Just do it.

Believe in yourself.

You must do it – there is no other option.

Keep going even when it's hard, always look after your kids, help them with your infinite heart, and just keep going until you have more pleasant moments than painful ones. Let's be honest: were you crying more before or after?

Be kind with yourself and find out how many abilities you have that you didn't even know about.

Write your own diary. Write about things you've done, your achievements, emotions, plans, and sorrows. So often, just seeing them all written down on a page, they suddenly seem clearer and more understandable.

And when you read those pages a year later, you will not believe the progress you've made.

Free your creativity, alone or with your kids, and your thoughts will start being more positive – and, therefore, your actions will as well.

Exercise at home and try to eat healthily. A happy body also means a happy mind, happy emotions,

SIGNED: A NORMAL SINGLE MOM

and a happy soul.

PLEASE do not look for help in a bottle of alcohol or in drugs. You will regret it so much the day after, and things will become even worse.

Singing out loud, maybe with the lyrics of your favourite playlist in front of the mirror, is way better! I do it and I love it.

Do you think that all other moms and dads go home every evening to an ideal super happy home? It's not always like that.

Comparing does not help, especially to imaginary facts. But living in the moment and accepting exactly where we are now –to the best of our abilities, creativity, and confidence – does.

If you do the job, do it not 'to make the other side wrong', but because you take complete responsibility for your kids' lives and wellbeing, and to become strong and feel valued.

I said at the beginning that I am not an expert, and this is not a 'how-to' book, but I thought that sharing things that were successful for me could be inspirational or helpful for someone else.

SIGNED: A NORMAL SINGLE MOM

I would love to know what you think about it, and if there is anything I can help you with.

CHAPTER THIRTY-FIVE

LET'S REFRAME EVERYTHING

I believe that a problem is only a problem based on the meaning we give it. For instance, the rain can be a problem for someone who resists it, and a blessing for someone who is hot and sweating.

Yes, you feel betrayed by people and life. You struggle with finding a balance between work and home, and with financial stress – which can be so intrinsic in your veins that you could not even conceive of living without it.

But that is only one side of the coin. Sometimes the only one people see. Or think it exists. Or 'the only way it has to be'.

But what about the other side, the bright one, where you cherish yours and your kids' achievements every day, and you are part of them? How blessed you are to enjoy that smile every day?

SIGNED: A NORMAL SINGLE MOM

What about the feeling of challenging yourself, and making it?

What about breaking old patterns, and see things from a completely new point of view? What about creating a new safe space, from which you can confidently create and prosper with your family?

Be kind with yourself, be brave and proud, and replace:

Failure with ACHIEVMENT

Self-doubt with CONFIDENCE

Struggle with DUTY

Frustration with MOTIVATION

Alone with TEAM

Loss with CHANCE

Abandoned with EMPOWERED

Fear with STRENGTH

Poor with CHALLANGING

Confused with CERTAINTY

Ideal with REAL

Past with PRESENT

Others with US

Pain with LOVE

SIGNED: A NORMAL SINGLE MOM

Tears with SMILE

Silence with CHATS

Injustice with FAIR

Suffering with RESPECT

Aaaahhh…now that feels better, doesn't it?

SIGNED: A NORMAL SINGLE MOM

SIGNED: A NORMAL SINGLE MOM

CHAPTER THIRTY-SIX

WHAT IF?

Through my open window, I can hear the seagulls flying above the sea. The temperature is perfect, and I am so grateful that you exist – and that I can write my book for you.

I am grateful for how things exist right here and right now, and for the blessing that is in every day.

Before thanking you for the precious time you chose to spend with me, I want to open the doors to new perspectives.

So, take some time to find an answer to each question:

What if you were a single mom in a different culture?

How could being a single mom not be a problem, but an asset instead?

What if you had ten kids to raise instead?

SIGNED: A NORMAL SINGLE MOM

What if your situation was worse than what it is?

How would your favourite hero deal with being a single mom?

How would 'you in ten years' respond to your current situation?

What advice would you give to a single mom coming to you for help?

What if… the best part of your life was still to come?

I hope that new lights have started to shine on you, and that a brighter, happier future is waiting for you and your beautiful family.

So, go out there and be the best version of yourself, for your kids' sake and yours. Our society needs heroes, not victims.

Thank you for sharing your time with me.

I hope I enriched your life in some way.

Thank you for your everyday hard work.

Do well.

Be You, Do You.

Because you are capable of amazing things.

SIGNED: A NORMAL SINGLE MOM

You are a smart woman and a fantastic mamma.

Now, let yourself be embraced by the warmth of that coffee, which is so well deserved.

With Love, Simo x

A Normal Single Mom

(If you want to answer some of my questions or get in touch, feel free to contact me at simothewriter@gmail.com. I would love to hear from You!)

SIGNED: A NORMAL SINGLE MOM

REFERENCE LIST

- DownDog App
- Kenny's Rock & Soul Café– 1A Kensington Gardens, Brighton, BN1 4AL
- Matt Rudnitsky, author of *'You Are An Author: So Write Your Book Already'*, rudbits.com
- Primark
- Sharon Blackie, author of *'The Enchanted Life'*
- Tablehurst Farm –London Road, Forest Row, RH18 5DP
- Drum and Blaze Samba Bateria Brighton_____

SIGNED: A NORMAL SINGLE MOM

SIGNED: A NORMAL SINGLE MOM

BIOGRAPHY

Simo is a happy and proud Italian single mom of four living on the south coast of England. She's now enjoying the life fulfilment her kids have achieved. But it has not always been like that.

Simo has desired to be a mom ever since she was a little girl playing with her doll, and now she is juggling motherhood with writing, life coaching, part-time jobs, acting classes, playing in a samba bateria, being passionate about the beauty and art all around her, keeping fit, being mistaken for her daughter's sister, her interest in life, helping others, being a lifelong traveller and the author of *'Per Te: Dall'Infinito'* (*To You: From Infinity*) published in Italy.

Simo encourages readers of this book to contact her at simothewriter@gmail.com.

SIGNED: A NORMAL SINGLE MOM

Printed in Great Britain
by Amazon